An easy household guide

by Nicky Scott

Illustrated by Axel Scheffler

Chelsea Green Publishing Company
White River Junction, Vermont

First published in 2004 by Green Books Ltd
Foxhole, Dartington
Totnes, Devon, TQ9 6EB, UK

Text © Nicky Scott 2004–7

Cartoons © Axel Scheffler 2004–7
axelscheffler@yahoo.co.uk

DISCLAIMER: The advice in this book about methods of
reusing and recycling is believed to be correct at the time of
printing, but readers should seek expert or professional advice if in
doubt about any of the recommendations made.

10 9 8 7 6 5 4 3 2 1   07 08 09 10

Printed in Canada

Printed on 100% postconsumer-waste recycled paper

First Chelsea Green printing July, 2007

Library of congress Cataloging-in-Publication Data
Scott, Nicky.
  Reduce, reuse, recycle : an easy household guide / by Nicky Scott ;
Illustrated by Axel Scheffler.
      p. cm.
  Includes bibliographical references.
  ISBN 978-1-933392-75-2
  1. Waste minimization. I. Title.

  TD793.9.S385 2007
  628.4—dc22

                                                    2007021452

Chelsea Green Publishing Company
P.O. Box 428
White River Junction, VT 05001
(802) 295-6300
www.chelseagreen.com

Contents

Acknowledgments

Amanda Cuthbert, for all those edits! Amy Griffiths, for setting me straight on the electrical issues; Paul Marten, MuRF manager from Exeter City Council, for reading various drafts and giving much of his considerable knowledge; Sam Seward for putting me straight on so many things—and for living the reduce, reuse, recycle lifestyle. Last but not least, John Elford at Green Books for asking me to write the book in the first place.

Introduction

This book will try to help you think about the contents of your garbage can in a new light. Hopefully, every time you go shopping it will give you some pause for thought. You will find yourself asking questions like: 'Where does this product come from? Is it made or grown locally? How many miles has it traveled? Can I buy it loose? Who made it? I hope they were well paid! Will it last? Is it made from recycled or recyclable materials? Can I recycle it or the packaging afterwards? Is it toxic? Is there a better alternative?'

For generations, we have been putting our garbage out to be taken away and buried in the ground in huge holes called landfill sites. The problem is that these huge holes are filling up faster and faster with increasing amounts of garbage. Landfill sites are being closed down, and getting planning to build new ones is very difficult—nobody wants to live next to a landfill site. They create toxic liquids and gases, which should be contained and dealt with, but inevitably accidents happen. Nobody wants to live near an incinerator either, and besides, they create toxic gases and ash. The ash needs to be safely disposed of—usually in a landfill.

As a society we are consuming more and more of the world's resources and generating more and more waste(d) materials. In the United States around a third of the contents of an average garbage can is material that ideally should be composted. At least another third is paper and cardboard that could be composted (although good clean paper can be recycled). Local authorities are under increasing pressure to cut down on the amounts being disposed of in landfill sites and incinerators. We need to aim for much higher recycling and composting rates, as well as work on changing our perceptions of what 'waste' is. Most of the 'stuff' we chuck away could be reused, repaired, recycled, or composted. It really is wasted! Future generations will no doubt be 'mining' landfill sites for valuable resources.

As well as trying to think about what to do with our garbage, we need to think about where all this garbage comes from in the first place. We can make a huge difference by refusing to buy things that will become a problem when they need to be disposed of. This is the main point of this book. By using the A-Z Guide, you can find lots of alternatives to throwing things in your garbage can.

More consumer items are being made now than ever before in the history of the planet. Many of them have an incredibly short life and are quickly discarded into the global garbage can, so try to buy items that are repairable.

There are more people on the planet than ever before, and we have evolved into a culture in which we are urged to consume more and more, with little or no regard for where our goods come from and how they are made. Shopping is now a major leisure activity and industry. And the attraction of a particular product depends to a large extent on how it is packaged.

The growing waste mountain

In the past, the make-up of the average garbage can was very different from what it is today. Most people had coal fires, so paper was used to start fires, and ash filled a large proportion of the garbage can; the Clean Air Act changed that. Fifty years ago there was virtually no plastic in the garbage can. There were no plastic 'blister' packs and very little processed food; most items were bought loose and wrapped in paper, and people went shopping with shopping baskets. There were returnable bottles, most people had their milk delivered, and other bottles had a deposit on them—a very useful addition to pocket money, and it kept the streets clear of bottles.

But change was on the way. With an ever more throwaway society, the amount we wasted grew, along with changes in the way we shopped and a massive increase in ever-more-alluring packaging. Reliance on processed food grew, which in turn meant even more packaging to throw away. The garbage trucks were just not big enough to keep up with our waste: new trucks had crushing and compacting mechanisms built into them.

Bottles were no longer returnable, and plastic was used for more and more items. Newspapers got bigger and bigger, processed food became mainstream, and the waste grew exponentially. The local town dumps were soon filled up. Huge incinerators were built, bigger landfill sites were dug, and still the waste grew. It became increasingly obvious to some environmentalists that the system would have to be changed—but with landfill being so cheap, it has been difficult to make reforms.

Recycling saves energy, saves natural resources, and reduces waste disposal. In a world of confusing messages, where environmental problems seem so huge that we as individuals cannot affect them, one of the easiest ways to have a positive impact on the world is to reduce our individual waste and to recycle and compost.

If you want to slim your garbage can, even just a little bit, here's a book that will help you. Every positive contribution, however small, is going to help. Give it a try—you can make a difference!

Chapter 1

Away with waste!

Reducing waste is the best option. It is staggering how much of what we throw away is perfectly good. A classic example of this is the increasing number of computers that are thrown out by large offices: when a whole system gets upgraded, often all the old ones are thrown into a dumpster. Yet old office computers can be reformatted with approved software and sold or donated to people on low incomes, community groups, etc.

Fashion also contributes to this waste; we have to have the latest stereo or electronic gizmo and dress in this year's colors. Some designers are now promoting 'anti-fashion' as a design concept that avoids temporary fashionable styles and promotes quality, durability, and less waste.

I recently saw a waste sanitation officer talking on a television program about waste. He said, "It's unbelievable the things that are brought to the dump. Don't these people have friends and neighbors they could talk to and offer their stuff to? It's a sad reflection on our society that we work to earn money to buy things with, which, particularly at the end of our lives, get buried in a hole in the ground, like us."

Reduce

Buy less stuff! Buy second-hand

Most of what we throw away could be used by other people. Thrift shops, tag sales, and flea markets do a great service in giving our unwanted items another lease on life—but so much more can be done.

Refuse packaging where possible

> *Roughly 30 cents of every dollar consumers spend on pack-aged goods goes toward paying for the packaging.*

Virtually every time we go shopping we are offered over-pack-aged items. These are then often put in another small plastic bag, and then a large plastic shopping bag. Get into the habit of refusing those bags! Carry your own shopping bags all the time—it's not difficult to have one or two in your pocket. Try to purchase loose items rather than prepacks or blisterpacks. In Germany, people routinely remove excess packaging at the checkout for the shop to sort out.

Buy quality goods when you can

One way to reduce the garbage you put in your garbage can is to buy better quality products. Avoid goods that won't last. Of course, unless you are very rich this is not always an option—at least not all the time—but nevertheless we all know that something really well made is going to outlast a cheaper, inferior product. Look for furniture in second-hand shops and auctions and pick up a bargain, before you dash off to buy something mass produced. Some designers now talk about anti-obsolescence: meaning designs that are easily repaired, maintained and upgraded so they are not made obsolete by changes of technology or taste.

Buy local, think global, and support your local economy

You may find that by shopping locally for fresh organic food you spend the same amount of money as you would getting in the car and driving to an out-of-town supermarket, and you also avoid packaging which is not recyclable. Likewise, the out-of-town home improvement superstore may sell cheaper paint, but are you thinking about how you could have painted half the wall in the time it takes you to get there and back?

- Consider buying local and handmade products. Support your local tradespeople. Well-crafted products are the heirlooms and antiques of the future. See www.onevillage.org
- If you are buying flat-pack, mass-produced furniture, look for the type that is sourced from sustainable forest management.
- A lot of flatpack furniture is made from composite materials. This is good in that some wood recycling is taking place and less space is taken up during transportation. Old pallets, for instance, can be chipped up and made into new products.

Avoid disposables

Try to avoid items that are used once and then thrown away—especially diapers, but also razors, cameras, plastic cutlery, cups and plates, and so on.

Avoid anything you can't reuse or recycle, where possible

Many household and garden chemicals should not be disposed of in the garbage and avoided, if possible. If you use materials that can be recycled or composted, you aren't left wondering what to do with a toxic substance.

Refill

Wherever possible, buy products in refillable containers. These include a range of soap products, dishwasher detergent, laundry detergent, all-purpose cleaner, cream cleaner, etc.

Some food shops also provide a wide range of loose food products (and they're often cheaper), so that you can take what you need with minimal packaging—even bring your own.

Buy in bulk

If you buy some of your food in bulk, you can:

- Decant or bottle up smaller quantities for use (which is cheaper in the long run)
- Join forces with friends and buy together and reduce the cost for all of you
- Have fun being creative with your bulk buys, such as marinating your own olives in oil with herbs and spices

Reuse

We are so used to throwing things away without a second thought, but we can:

Repair Furniture is often thrown away when it could be given a whole new lease of life in the hands of a local craftsman.

Reinstate Chairs can be re-caned, sofas and chairs re-upholstered.

Reactivate A rusty chain on a bike can often be rejuvenated by soaking in penetrating oil, as can other rusty machine parts. Of course, bicycle chains would not have to be reactivated if they had been regularly oiled in the first place!

Reinvent Find new uses for everyday items: e.g., plastic drink bottles make great mini-cloches/cold frames to protect tender plants from slugs.

Donate Give things to thrift shops, flea markets, hospitals, playgroups, residential homes, etc.

Many thrift shops are now becoming extremely good at marketing a whole range of products. The CDs that used to be put in a box on the floor are now being displayed as they would be in a music shop. Some thrift shops are becoming specialists in particular areas: designer clothes can now be purchased at thrift shops, whereas others specialize in 'retro,' with old telephones selling alongside 1950s and 60s china and furnishing fabrics. Some specialize in books, others in furniture, and so on. Browsing in thrift shops is becoming positively trendy!

In some cities, people put useful items out on the sidewalk the evening before the garbage collection, and whole streets turn into free flea markets. In New York, anything left on the sidewalk soon disappears. It even works in the small town where I live, so I'm sure it's an idea that could catch on anywhere.

Sell So much of the stuff that gets taken to recycling centers or thrown out can be sold. Swap meets are excellent for this— make some money! Auction houses will also sell anything from prime pieces of furniture to miscellaneous boxes with the most unlikely assortment of odds and ends. And nowadays there are auction sites on the Internet, such as eBay.

Recycle

Recycling in this country is still in its infancy. We have a long way to go, but soon everyone in the country will be offered a doorstep collection for at least some of the materials that could be recycled. Some parts of the country that have been recycling for longer have achieved far higher recycling rates than average.

They are now moving into extending the range of materials recycled, for example, by collecting kitchen and garden waste for composting, and plastics.

Get into the habit

In the U.S. we have gone from very little recycling to a national average of nearly 30%.

More and more areas are offering curbside collections for recyclable materials, making changing our habits easy. You can really help your municipality by checking what they will or will not accept for recycling in your area. Different municipalities operate different systems: some have bags, others use boxes or special garbage cans. If you have a recycling box, it helps to put cans, cardboard, and newspapers/magazines into separate bags within the box.

Clean garbage

Recycling depends on having clean, separated material—for instance putting china in with glass bottles can lead to whole loads of glass being rejected. It is becoming a part of our daily life to rinse out our bottles, jars, and cans for recycling. Most of us have easy access to at least the more common recycling centers for glass, newspapers and magazines, cans, and clothes.

Recycling bulky items

Many counties are busy improving their sites where people can take 'bulky' household waste. Anything from old sofas, bikes, baths, and bricks to woody prunings, branches, plastic bottles, glass, waste oil, and timber. These facilities are undergoing a face-lift so that more and more is saved rather than being buried or burned.

Contact your local sanitation department to find out where your nearest recycling facility is and what you can or cannot take there. Alternatively, you may have a local community-operated organization—if so, contact them first!

Buy Recycled

Purchase items made from recycled products: they are becoming better all the time as more and more of us seek them out. See *www.amazingrecycled.com*

Compost

Home composting is great—it's just about the only reprocessing that we can all do and it removes so much from the garbage can. Nearly two-thirds of our garbage consists of material that could be composted, and much of that is paper and cardboard.

On average, each one of us produces 4.4 pounds of solid waste each day. This adds up to almost a ton of trash per person per year.

Chapter 2

Some recycling myths

There are a number of arguments that are all too often levied at recycling—for example, that it uses more energy and is more expensive than using raw materials. This is untrue (see below).

Critics of recycling also cite examples like transporting glass hundreds of miles to be melted down. Of course, there are still some undoubtedly unsustainable practices like this, and we need to develop more localized reprocessing facilities, markets, and uses for all the materials that we recycle, but in fact this is just one of several recycling myths.

Statistics are sometimes used to show the economics of recycling in a bad light, but they fail to take into account the hidden costs of, for example, cleaning up the pollution caused by landfills, mining, and transporting the raw materials.

The Myths

1. "There's no point in recycling because all the stuff just gets dumped."

This is a common story in the press. What is often not realized is that just a single Pyrex® dish or piece of china in the glass recycle bin will contaminate the whole load and make it unusable. The vast majority of loads are fine and end up being reprocessed, but unfortunately bad media stories tend to stay in the mind longer than good ones.

Recycling is worthwhile and is getting better all the time as more and more people put out clean, sorted material for recycling, and as the technology to sort mechanically improves.

A visit to a Materials Recycling Facility or 'MuRF' is fascinating. MuRFs can sort some of the plastics out mechanically. In some of them you can see completely unsorted materials coming in. Bags are split open and the contents travel along conveyor belts where they are jiggled, tumbled through huge revolving drums, passed under powerful magnets, blown with air knives, and zapped with laser beams. These beams can identify the types of plastic and then jets of air blast the item down the appropriate chute. All these processes can do the major sorting out of materials—the lighter materials from the heavier, the steel from the aluminum, the small from the large, and there is also a certain amount of handpicking as well.

2. "It costs more to recycle than to make things from new materials."
This is not true. Many recycled products not only save energy and water but also reduce raw-material usage and the associated energy and pollution caused in the process of obtaining the raw materials. For example, it is far better to be constantly recycling aluminum than wastefully mining out the finite stocks of bauxite and causing unnecessary pollution and wasting energy in the process.

3. "It costs more to recycle than it does to throw trash away."
Trash collection costs us all money, but the real cost has been disguised due to subsidized landfill costs. With landfills filling up and closing down and landfill taxes having been introduced in a number of areas, recycling makes more and more financial sense.

Manufacturing 1 ton of recycled paper results in 74% less air pollution and 43% less water pollution compared to the manufacture of paper using virgin wood pulp.

4. "It causes huge amounts of pollution trucking all the recyclable materials around the country."
It is true that there are relatively few reprocessors for recyclable materials at the present and that mileage costs and associated pollution have to be taken into account. However, as more uses and markets are developed and more local reprocessing takes place, the market price for recycled materials will rise.

5. "Washing out cans and bottles uses more energy than is saved by recycling them."
Not if you wash them out at the end of doing the dishes!

6. "It all takes up to much time, and I don't have enough space."
You will need to dedicate a container for recyclable materials, but you will be saving space in your garbage can and maybe even need one less can. Once you are into the swing of recycling, it takes very little time.

7. "You have to take all the labels off—it's all too much trouble."
Labels don't have to be removed from bottles or cans, but food containers do need to be rinsed out.

8. *"There's so much green glass that it just gets thrown away."*
Only contaminated loads of glass ever get thrown away (see 1 above). However, new uses have to be found for materials like glass so that a more competitive marketplace is established. There are now dozens of alternative uses for glass—see 'glass' in the **A-Z Guide**.

9. *"Recycled products are poor quality."*
Products made from recycled materials are every bit as good as (if not better than) products made from raw materials. For example, throughout the world, military and commercial aircraft use retread tires, and this is in an area where safety is paramount. See *www.greenshop.co.uk*

Aluminum and glass and some plastics can be recycled indefinitely without a loss in quality. Paper, however, can be recycled only a limited number of times because the fibers get shorter and shorter, but it can be reprocessed into other products. Many paper processors mix fresh, long fibers with reprocessed paper to make new paper.

10. *"Recycled products are too expensive."*
Not always! However, the market is new, and creating demand for products using recycled materials is important and will help to lower prices in the longer term.

Chapter 3

A–Z Guide

Aerosols

REDUCE / *Avoid:* To avoid contributing to the growth of the hole in the ozone layer, try to use an alternative. Use pump sprays instead of aerosol cans.

RECYCLE Can be recycled when empty, but check with your local authority first (DO NOT SQUASH or pierce—they can explode).

Aluminum

RECYCLE Wash and squash cans first. Aluminum is the most valuable of our commonly recycled materials and is one of the most important items to keep out of your trash can.

Sell or Donate: Large items, cooking pans, window frames, etc., can be taken to a scrap dealer or recycling center.

Aluminum Foil and Containers

REDUCE Aluminum foil is useful stuff, but you don't have to use it to wrap everything you put in the oven or fridge, and you don't have to wrap up sandwiches in it. Use a paper bag or wax paper.

REUSE it as much as possible, clean, flatten, and put it back in the drawer for next time. Containers can be used for seed trays.

RECYCLE many local recycling programs will collect it for recycling—it needs to be collected separately from aluminum cans and pans but can still be reprocessed.

Antifreeze

RECYCLE *Donate:* Give it to your neighbor or local mechanic.

Appliances—see Electrical and Electronic Appliances

Asbestos

Asbestos is a very dangerous substance: when disturbed in any way, it releases carcinogenic fibers into the air. If you think you may have asbestos that is going to be disturbed or you wish to remove, contact your local authority for advice before doing anything.

Disposal There are three types of asbestos: white, brown, and blue. However, do not rely on the color for identification: contact your local authority for advice. Do not attempt to remove or repair asbestos without getting advice from an expert. Do not take asbestos to a recycling center.

You must ensure that arrangements are made to dispose of the material prior to removal. There are specific guidelines for commercial contractors to dispose of materials correctly.

Ash

REUSE charcoal for garden paths, or make a narrow path across your lawn for the winter.

RECYCLE *Compost:* Wood ash can be sprinkled lightly into your compost heap or around your garden. It is also used by potters in glazes and in soap making.

DISPOSE—coal ash should be disposed of in your trash can.

Attic Clearance

Think first! What can you sell or donate or recycle? Try selling, as well. EBay and Craig's List have huge audiences just waiting to buy your junk! See *www.ebay.com* or *www.craigslist.com*

Autumn Leaves

RECYCLE *or Compost:* Put wet autumn leaves in a plastic bag, stab a fork in to make some holes, and a year later you'll have compost. Even better, pick the leaves off the lawn with a mower, which will mix grass cuttings and chop the leaves up, and you'll have compost even more quickly. Don't burn leaves, as they produce highly carcinogenic smoke—particularly bad for babies and children—and it's a waste of all that lovely material.

Baby Goods

RECYCLE *Sell or Donate:* Good-condition clothes and equipment can go to second-hand shops and thrift shops. Contact your local playgroup or nursery school—put up a card on their noticeboard.

Bags—see Plastic Bags

Barrels (Beer, Wine, etc.)

REUSE Contact the original supplier of the barrels: they can be reused. If too far gone to hold liquid (the barrel, not you) then *Sell* or saw in half to make plant containers.

Bathroom Fittings and Furniture

REUSE Sinks, waste pipes, and even old toilets can be used for plants: a sink in the ground is useful for containing mint and other invasive plants.
Sell or Donate: Advertise locally, sell to architectural salvage yards, or give to recycling centers.

Batteries (Car)

RECYCLE Nearly 90 percent of all lead-acid batteries are recycled. Almost any retailer that sells car batteries collects used batteries for recycling, as required by most state laws. Reclaimers crush batteries into nickel-sized pieces and separate the plastic components. They send the plastic to a reprocessor for manufacture into new plastic products and deliver purified lead to battery manufacturers and other industries. A typical lead-acid battery contains 60 to 80 percent recycled lead and plastic.

Batteries (Household)

The energy needed to manufacture a battery is on average 50 times greater than the energy it gives out.

REDUCE Cut down on batteries—use the sun! Buy solar powered (or clockwork) equipment. Otherwise, use rechargeable batteries and a battery charger. You can now get CD or cassette tape walkmans, radios, flashlights and toothbrushes which use rechargeable batteries.
See *www.freeenergynews.com*

RECYCLE The U.S. is relatively ahead of the game for the recycling of batteries. The Battery Act of 1996 was created to phase out the use of mercury in batteries and provide for the efficient and cost-effective collection and recycling or proper disposal of used nickel cadmium batteries, small sealed lead-acid batteries, and certain other batteries. In addition there is a national program, Call2Recycle™, sponsored by the Rechargeable Battery Recycling Corporation (RBRC) to help you recycle your used portable rechargeable batteries and old cell phones. See *www.rbrc.org*

Why recycle batteries? While the exact chemical make-up varies in different types, most batteries contain heavy metals that are a cause for environmental concern. When disposed of incorrectly, these heavy metals may leak into the ground when the battery casing corrodes. This can contribute to soil and water pollution and endanger wildlife. Cadmium, for example, can be toxic to aquatic invertebrates and can accumulate in fish, which makes them unfit for human consumption. Some batteries, such as button-cell batteries, also contain mercury, which has similarly hazardous properties. Mercury is no longer being used in the manufacture of non-rechargeable batteries, except button cells where it is a functional component.

Batteries
(Button cell—hearing aid, camera, watch, calculator, etc.)

REDUCE Buy a wind-up watch or use a solar-powered calculator.

RECYCLE Some distributors will accept batteries for their valuable oxides of silver and mercury, especially photography shops and jewelers.

Bedding and Blankets

RECYCLE *Sell or Donate:* Thrift shops will sell clean, good-quality bedding, etc., and you can also reuse it for rags, dust sheets, etc.—see **Textiles**.

RECYCLE *Compost:* Pure wool, cotton, linen, and other natural fibers can be composted. However, you cannot compost manmade fibers, or natural materials if mixed with manmade fibers.

Beds

RECYCLE *Sell or Donate:* to furniture projects, social services, or your local recycling center. Mattresses can be reused only if they conform to current fire safety standards.

Beverage Cartons—see Cartons

Bicycles

RECYCLE metals for scrap value.

Sell or Donate: Advertise locally or use auction sales, flea markets, or swap meets. Bicycle shops will often refurbish your bike for resale or dismantle it for spare parts.

A number of charities either rebuild bicycles or collect old ones and send them to developing countries.

See *www.bikesfortheworld.org*

Don't leave them outside in the rain to rust! (See page 14.)

Birthdays—see Christmas

Blockboard

REUSE take to a recycling center for reuse. You should not burn composite woods like blockboard because of the resins and glues, which are toxic.

Books

REDUCE Use your local library.

RECYCLE Some organizations and charities also have book banks for recycling books back into paper.

Sell or Donate: Books in good condition can often be sold to secondhand bookshops—otherwise donate to thrift shops, etc.

Bottles and Jars

The energy saved from recycling one glass bottle will operate a 100-watt light bulb for four hours.

REUSE Try to buy reusable/refillable ones. Jars and bottles also have many reuses apart from recycling. Lids can be attached to the underside of shelves, and the jar can be screwed in having been filled with nails or screws, etc. I use jam jars for small amounts of glaze that I need to test for my annual marmalade-making session (not the same ones, of course!) And they can be used for all manner of small amounts of foodstuffs, paint, etc.

RECYCLE Remember to remove the lids: if you mix metal and glass, the load could be rejected and sent to the landfill. The lids can go with the tins and cans.

Bric-a-brac

RECYCLE *Sell or Donate:* Save for garage sales, thrift shops, swap meets, etc.

Bricks

REUSE Can be cleaned for reuse. Bricks have masses of uses in the garden, supporting rain barrels, troughs, etc., for paths, raised beds, and of course new building projects.

RECYCLE at a Recycling Center.
Sell or Donate: Advertise locally.

Brochures—see Catalogs

Brushes

REDUCE Paint brushes last longer if you look after them:
- Buy good-quality paintbrushes and clean them carefully.
- If you are going to use them again soon, put brushes from oil-based paints in water to the top of the bristles to stop them from drying out. Load emulsion paintbrushes and rollers up with plenty of paint and put in a pot (or tray) with a plastic bag over the top.
- When you have finished, wipe brushes on newspaper first—use a small amount of mineral spirits for oil brushes

and then use more newspaper. For emulsion brushes, use hot water and a spot of detergent.

- Keep brushes used for black paint just for black paint jobs.

REUSE Toothbrushes can be reused for all kinds of cleaning jobs. Trim the ends of any gummed-up brushes with scissors for new life.

B

Bubble Wrap

REUSE It's very therapeutic to pop it, and it keeps my daughter occupied for hours. However, local potters and craft shops, etc., can reuse if it's big enough, and unpopped! Wrap plants and plant pots in it to protect them from frost. Use it for transporting breakable items when moving or for wrapping things before sending them through the mail.

Building Materials

REUSE *Sell or Donate:* These make up a huge part of the waste problem. Any decent quantity of stuff is worth advertising in the local paper—alternatively, you may have a local community project or reclamation yard. When undertaking building work it pays to set up a clear system so that materials can be separated out: wood, bricks, blocks, rubble, mortar, metals, wiring and cables, plastics, windows and doors, etc. Also see under individual headings.

If you are renovating your house:

- Bricks can be reused, e.g., in the garden
- Any large pieces of stone can be incorporated into garden design
- Metals and cables can be sold to a scrap dealer
- Doors and windows can go to an architectural salvage yard
- Wood can be reused or burned
- Mortar and old plaster can be bagged up for reuse in the garden
- Rubble can form the base of paths or tracks

Modern houses tend to be made with
many more manmade materials that
are not easily recycled: PVC windows, doors, gutters, etc., composite woods bound with resins, foam
insulation and so on. When these
buildings are demolished in the
future, there will be fewer useful
recyclable or reusable materials.

For reclaimed building materials see *www.salvoweb.com*

Building Rubble

RECYCLE *Sell or Donate:* If you are planning any building
projects you might need some rubble: store it in a corner until
needed. It is also useful for landscaping foundations in the
garden. You could advertise locally: give it away free to anyone willing to take it away, or as a last resort take to a recycling center.

Bulky Refuse

RECYCLE Many charities offer a household collection service, but make sure it really is unwanted or unusable by anyone else first before you contact them.

Cameras—see Disposable Single-Use Cameras

Everyday 80 million food and drink cans end up in landfills.

Cans—see also Aluminum

RECYCLE Rinse cans at the end of your dishwashing and
recycle. Aluminum cans are the most cost-effective materials
to recycle, so don't waste them! Recycled aluminum from
cans is used extensively to make new products.

   Steel cans are also valuable and well worth recycling. They

are easily separated from the aluminum with magnets at the Materials Reclamation Facility. On average, every single person in America uses 142 steel cans each year.

Cardboard

REUSE Large cardboard sheets are useful in the garden as a weed-suppressing mulch. Ideally, cover them with compost.

RECYCLE Shred it for animal bedding. Many recycling organizations will collect or accept cardboard, which then gets sent for reprocessing.

Compost: Cardboard is great for compost heaps, worms love it! Either line your heaps with it or rip it up or just put in layers with wet green material like grass cuttings—see also Compost section below.

Cardboard tubes: Apart from composting or recycling, cardboard tubes have many reuse applications. A designer in Denmark has designed a clever way to link together cardboard tubes so that a roll-up screen can be made from them. A Japanese designer has gone even further and uses tubes for a whole range of furniture.

Cards

RECYCLE Greetings cards are recycled along with cardboard by some municipalities, so check to see if they are accepted in your area.

Carpets

REUSE Make a carpetbag!

Clean: Many carpets are disposed of simply because they are dirty! Hiring an industrial-strength steam cleaner for the weekend can transform your carpets, and kill any clothes moths that may have taken up residence. If the moths have taken hold, woolen carpets and felt underlay can be used as a mulch material in the garden or allotment. There are many companies who specialize in carpet cleaning and refurbishment if you don't want to do it yourself.

Replace: Another option for carpets, common in offices, is to use carpet squares, which can then be replaced individually as necessary.

Sell or Donate: Offer them to social services, hostels, local schools, scrapstores, etc., or advertise locally.

Recycled carpets One of the Web sites I stumbled across in researching this book was *www.carpet-burns.com*. Recycled carpet is molded into hard, durable 3D forms, or processed into a hard board material, by combining heat and pressure. The carpet then assumes new properties and becomes waterproof, oilproof, and highly durable, with a smooth surface. All kinds of novel techniques like this are springing up to deal with a wide range of products that would previously have been thrown away.

Cars and Spare Tires

RECYCLE *Sell or Donate:* Failing that, you should always take end-of-life vehicles to an auto salvage yard, where useful parts are removed for reuse or sale (if you are feeling strong, you could do it yourself). Old and unusual vehicles will usually have their own dedicated clubs who will often take your vehicle and lovingly restore it. Useful spare tires can be advertised or your local garage may well be happy to take them.

See *www.zyra.org.uk/scrapcar.htm*

Cartons

REDUCE Avoid where possible.

REUSE Cartons can be used as plant pots—on their sides for seedlings and upright for single plants.

RECYCLE Recycling is becoming an option for waxed beverage or soup cartons, which are also often lined with plastic or foil. A few curbside collection services are collecting cartons. See *www.tetrapak.com,* and also see *www.cutouts.net* to see how tetra packs are turned into mouse pads and clipboards.

Cartridges (inkjet, laser, etc.)—see Toner Cartridges

Catalogs
RECYCLE They can go with newspapers and magazines for recycling.

Cat Litter
RECYCLE *Compost:* Cat litter can be added to the compost heap—however, it is best to bury or dispose of any cat feces first, to avoid the risk of spreading parasites.

You can now buy cat litter made from recycled paper, hemp, and mineral sources—for example, bentonite clay.

CDs and DVDs
REUSE
- Hang in the garden as bird scarers.
- Use as reflectors in your drive.
- Cut up and stick to a ball to make a disco ball!
- Use as coasters for drinks.
- Sell to record shops.
- Donate to a local scrapstore or thrift shop for reuse

RECYCLE Some firms now collect CDs and their cases for recycling. Try Ne-sar Systems (412) 827-8172. See also www.greendisk.com

Cellophane
Genuine cellophane is derived from cellulose and is biodegradable. Some food products are still wrapped in it, but most so-called cellophane is in fact polypropylene and not biodegradable. The only way to tell is either to contact

the manufacturers or to try to compost it. See **Envelopes** for where to buy genuine cellophane window envelopes.
See *www.pak-sel.com/sub1.htm*

Ceramics and China

REUSE Broken china can be utilized in mosaic work. Mosaics are becoming more common in civic spaces. Ceramics can also be ground up for incorporation into new building blocks. Put up a notice at your local crafts center or advertise locally if you have a quantity of interesting broken ceramics.

Never put ceramics, old drinking glasses, or Pyrex® in with glass for recycling as it will contaminate the entire load and will have to be sent to the landfill. Put it in your trash can if you don't want to reuse it.

Some incredible work has been produced using ceramics: see the work of Gaudi in Barcelona, where there are whole buildings covered in ceramic pieces, or Niki de Saint Phalle's *Tarot Garden* in Tuscany, and the work of Nek Chand in India. See *www.nikidesaintphalle.com* *www.nekchand.com*

Cereal Boxes

RECYCLE Your area may collect cardboard.
Compost: Best to flatten then rip or scrunch before adding to the heap.

REUSE Playgroups and nurseries often collect cardboard tubes and boxes for 'creative play.' See also **Children**.

CFCs (Chlorofluorocarbons)—see Fridges and Freezers

Chemicals—see also Garden Chemicals

By chemicals we generally mean hazardous or toxic substances used in the household, which include paint, mineral spirits, bleach, antifreeze, brake fluid, engine oil, garden and household chemicals, woodworm treatments, and so on. Some of these are listed in this A-Z Guide, but if in doubt, contact your local authority for disposal advice.

REDUCE Try to find alternatives to the most toxic ones—check the labels.

Disposal Never dispose of chemicals down the sink or drain. Unwanted pesticides and other garden chemicals must be disposed of properly—all hazardous substances should be taken to a recycling center for safe disposal. Contact your local authority first for advice.

For a comprehensive database of household chemicals, The Household Products Database of the National Library of Medicine links over 6,000 consumer brands to health effects from Material Safety Data Sheets (MSDS) and allows scientists and consumers to research products based on chemical ingredients. See *www.householdproducts.nlm.nih.gov*

Children

I'm not suggesting that we should recycle children! Children really like the idea of recycling (and composting) and it's never too early to introduce them to it. A lot of the materials we throw away are essential components in craft constructions. When children are feeling creative, it's great to have boxes of materials on hand, for example:

* cardboard boxes and tubes, plastic bottles and yogurt cups plus glue, string, and silver foil

- jam jars (for older children) and tins with lids can hold small items like buttons, bottle caps, nails, screws, odds and ends
- pieces of material with thread, cord, ribbons and wire for fastening things
- paper used on one side and pieces of cardboard for painting and gluing pictures to
- magazines and catalogs with pictures of animals, trucks, landscapes, flowers, etc., to cut up for collages

If you find you're collecting too much, try offering it to your local school, playgroup, or nursery.

For a bit of fun, try putting a potato chip bag in the oven at a low temperature—it shrinks to a fraction of its full size. It's fascinating to see a miniature of the product with all the writing barely legible.

Chipboard

REUSE Keep dry for reuse, as otherwise it will swell up and be useless.

Dispose Chipboard contains toxic glues and resins, so do not burn: dispose of small bits in a trash can, or take to a recycling center for disposal.

Christmas

REDUCE You can reduce your Christmas waste by:

- Trying to really think about the presents you buy and trying to purchase them locally and ethically
- Buying cards made from recycled cards
- Supporting your local shops and craftspeople
- Reusing good quality wrapping paper
- Recycling old Christmas cards

REUSE You can cut up Christmas cards to reuse as either new cards or gift tags. Most Christmas decorations get reused year after year.

Don't put cards in the newspaper and magazine recycling bins, as card fiber cannot be recycled into paper, but it can go in any cardboard collection you may have.

RECYCLE Paper chains and other paper and card decorations can go for recycling along with cardboard, but broken glass balls should be wrapped in paper and put in the trash can. For more ideas go to *www.mindfully.org* and search on Christmas—it's a great site!

Christmas Trees

RECYCLE *Compost:* Many areas now offer Christmas tree collection points. The trees are shredded for composting or used for stabilizing sand dunes. You may have a local community composting project which will take it.

Cleaning—see also Chemicals

REDUCE Avoid harsh chemical cleaners: you can use cleaners (for all household uses, including yourself and your clothes) made from natural products and even use a steam cleaner—then you won't have to dispose of any hazardous chemicals.

Clingfilm/Plastic Wrap

REDUCE Plastic wrap is useful stuff, but there's no need to wrap everything in it! Try putting food in a bowl in the fridge with a plate over it instead. Plastic wrap cannot yet be recycled.

Clothing—see also Textiles

REDUCE The fashion industry wants us to constantly change our clothes, and huge quantities of clothing are discarded as a result: do you really need that new sweater?

REUSE

- Some businesses make completely new clothing from old.
- Children love dressing up both themselves and their dolls and teddy bears—keep a box of clothes handy.
- Contact your local amateur theater group.

Sell or Donate: Good clean clothing can be reused: take it to garage sales, thrift shops, or put in clothing donation boxes. Even if it cannot be reused as clothing, it can be recycled into paper and textiles. Designer labels can be sold through consignment shops.

RECYCLE Some scraps of material are wanted by quiltmakers. If you have even quite small pieces of (especially) small print material, they will put it to good use. Advertise locally or in a craft shop, or contact the American Quilter's Society.

See *www.americanquilter.com*

What happens to my old clothes?

When textiles are recycled:

- 35% of reclaimed textiles are reused as second-hand clothing
- 33% are converted into fiber to be used in new textile products
- 25% become wiping and polishing cloths
- 7% end up in landfill

Textile recyclers are capable of delivering a pair of pants in clean, damage-free condition to the east coast of Africa for $.34 a pair and sweaters to Pakistan for $.12 each. While a few communities have textile-recycling programs, about 85 percent of this waste goes to landfills where it occupies about 4 percent of landfill space. See the Council for Textile Recycling at www.textilerecycle.org

Coat Hangers

REUSE *Donate*: Thrift shops and dry cleaners often need hangers.

RECYCLE Some curbside recycling programs accept wire hangers; check with your local authority.

Coffins—see Funerals

Coins

REUSE AND **RECYCLE**

Donate: U.S. and foreign coins can be given to charities.

- Coinstar machines convert your coins to cash for a fee but also allow you to donate directly to charity. See *www.coin-star.com*
- Banks, post offices, and other shops sometimes collect your foreign coins for recirculation or to give to charity.

Sell: to collectors or to specialist shops.

Compost

REDUCE Make it yourself, but if you have to buy it, buy it locally. You may be lucky enough to have a community composting group or composting business in your area who will be able to take your garden waste.

Don't buy peat-based composts or growing medium. See **Peat**.

RECYCLE The growing media from old hanging baskets and grow bags, etc., can be spread around the garden or added to a compost heap.

To find out more about composting, see *Composting: An Easy Household Guide* in the **Resources** section.

Computers

REUSE Many recycling projects and commercial companies will take computers, monitors, and associated hardware. They can wipe hard drives with special software and resell equipment to low-income groups, etc. Even broken equipment can be taken apart for components.

If you work in an office, tell your manager about these services before your whole system is upgraded and the old computers are junked. Check out E-cycling Central for where to recycle electronics in your area. See *www.iae.org*

Sell or Donate: Recycles.org serves as a regional and nationwide exchange board directly connecting those wishing to dispose of computers and nonprofit organizations in need. See *www.recycles.org*

Cooking oil

REUSE Biodiesel projects are springing up around the country—imagine powering your car on french fry oil! If you have a local community recycling project, they should be able to tell you more. See an example of a biofuel project at *www.rapoleum.com*

Old oil can also be used to add life to wooden garden furniture, wooden compost bins, etc. (thin with paraffin first). Also, try having a container with sand and oil that you clean garden forks and spades in: it cleans and oils at the same time!

RECYCLE *Compost:* If you really can't find a use for it, then oil can be composted. It's best to mix well with paper or cardboard first. See *www.biodiesel.org*

Copper

RECYCLE *Sell:* Copper pipes and hot-water cylinders are often dumped, but they are valuable and can be reused or reprocessed. Take to a scrap metal dealer or recycling site.

Corks

REUSE Corks are not being recycled at the moment, but their time will come! In the meantime they have some re-uses:

- You can use them for lighting fires or for soundproofing (they're sometimes used in bars).
- Use as infill between wooden supports to make little soundproof booths—it works!
- You can make cork noticeboards from whole corks by gluing them together in a frame.
- Put them on the end of sharp tools such as utility knives.

Cork facts

- Cork recycled from wine bottles can be used to make products such as place mats, floor tiles, gaskets, fishing rods, shoe edges, and insulation material.
- Countries including Australia, Germany, Belgium, and Switzerland have cork recycling programs. In Australia, the Girl Guides collect tons of corks every year to raise funds—we could easily do it here too.
- Since its launch in February 2003, the Cork Information Bureau in the UK claims to have has seen a fivefold increase in the number of inquiries received about cork recycling. It says these inquiries have come from a mix of local authorities, businesses, the wine trade, and individual consumers.
- Real corks are preferable to plastic corks for many reasons, the main one being that cork forests in Portugal and Spain support an incredible diversity of wildlife.
- Cork trees are now protected by the Portuguese government as a renewable resource, and the average lifespan of a cork tree is more than 200 years.
- Real corks are easier to get out of the bottle and off the corkscrew and can be recycled or composted.

See *www.corkfacts.com*

Crockery—see Ceramics and China

Curtains

RECYCLE *Sell:* There is a growing market for second-hand curtains on eBay.
Donate: to thrift shops.

D

Cutlery

Sell or Donate: to thrift shops, swap meets, etc.

Diapers

> *The average baby goes through 5,000 diapers*
> *before being potty-trained;*
> *8 million diapers are thrown out every day.*

REDUCE Try to use disposable diapers only for when you are traveling or cannot use reusable ones.

REUSE Disposable diapers will take hundreds of years to decompose in landfill sites. However, new biodegradable brands such as Seventh Generation, Nature Boy & Girl, and TenderCare Plus provide a better alternative. Nature Boy & Girl diapers are made of cornstarch instead of plastic. And unlike regular disposable diapers, TenderCare Plus and Seventh Generation diapers are not bleached in chlorine, a process that emits toxins into the air and water.

There are a number of great cloth diapering options that have become popular, such as the all-in-one—a diaper cover with a washable cloth insert. Diaper services are also an option if you cannot launder them at home.

Disposable Items

These are generally not recyclable, so try to avoid them.

Disposable Single-use Cameras

*Despite the recycling claims on the boxes,
fewer than 50% of disposable cameras are recycled.*

REDUCE Avoid disposable single-use cameras. You can buy inexpensive fully automatic 35mm cameras, which will give better results and cost less to use than disposables. Alternatively, buy a digital camera and view your pictures on screen.

RECYCLE If you do buy a disposable camera, be sure to take it to a developer who explicitly promises to recycle the remains.

Dog and Cat Poo

RECYCLE This can be put in a sealed Solarcone: see under **Food: Meat and Fish.** Otherwise, wrap in paper and dispose of in garbage can or bury in your garden. As dog and cat feces can contain parasites, keep away from children and always wash your hands after dealing with it.

Drink Cans—see Cans

Egg Cartons

REUSE They can sometimes be reused by the producer. Otherwise, compost cardboard ones, or offer them to play groups, scrapstores, schools, or outlets that sell eggs from the garden gate.

Compost: They are good for the compost heap.

Electrical and Electronic Appliances

REDUCE Use wind-up or solar appliances where possible, e.g., radios and calculators (see under **Batteries**). Then you can listen to the radio during power failures, or when you are working in the garden, without using batteries.

REUSE / *Repair:* Lots of electrical equipment is thrown away just because it is old and outdated. Local community recycling and furniture projects will advise you what to do with your unwanted equipment: much of it can be repaired and reused, and many of these projects employ qualified electricians to approve any repair work.

RECYCLE Many retailers will take back any electrical and electronic items bought from them. Electrical and electronic equipment contains hazardous substances that need to be taken out, reprocessed, and reused.

Electricity

REDUCE reliance on the grid. Electricity comes largely from burning fossil fuels, which contributes to global warming. Use wind-up or solar-powered devices wherever possible. Change your energy provider to one who uses green energy. Compare suppliers and save money too!

Energy

Reduce your energy use: save yourself money in the long run and your footprint on the planet.

Every day more solar energy falls on the Earth than the total amount of energy than the planet's 5.9 billion inhabitants would consume in 27 years.

See *www.myfootprint.org www.greenenergychoice.com www.greenmountainenergy.com* or contact your local utility provider for help.

Engine Oil

It takes just one quart of engine oil to pollute 185,000 gallons of fresh water.

RECYCLE You can often take engine oil to a recycling center, service station, or quick-lube shop. See *www.recycleoil.org* or *www.earth911.org* for recycling locations throughout the country. Emptying used oil into storm drains can cause real harm to the environment; just one gallon of used oil can contaminate 740,000 gallons of water.

Envelopes

REUSE Envelopes can sometimes not be recycled because of the glue (although some municipalities take them). If not, they can easily be reused: stick on reuse labels, which are readily available, or remove the windows and compost them. Some recycling will not accept brown or paper-padded envelopes. Similarly, plastic envelopes and those with plastic bubble padding are very difficult to recycle. Purchasing white or light-colored envelopes—and those without plastic windows—increases the chance that you will be able to recycle them.

Fabrics—see Clothing, Textiles

Faxes—see Junk Mail

Flip-Flops

Thousands of flip-flops end up being washed up on beaches: one project in Kenya is making a range of products from them. See *www.flipflopalula.com.*

Fluorescent Light Tubes (also see Light bulbs)

RECYCLE These contain toxic mercury, which can be safely recovered. For a comprehensive primer on recycling mercury-containing lamps, see Lamprecycle.org *www.lamprecycle.org*

Foil—see Aluminum Foil

Food

REDUCE Try to minimize food waste:

- Incorporate leftovers in other meals, and boil up bones for stock
- Most fruit and vegetables are designed by nature to keep for weeks or months in the right conditions (in the cool and out of direct light)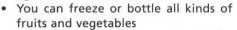
- You can freeze or bottle all kinds of fruits and vegetables
- If you grow your own food, there are all kinds of ways of storing food for long periods, including drying, fermenting, and bottling

REUSE

- Dogs have their uses—relishing your leftovers.
- Stale bread is never wasted in Italy: it can be made into croutons or used in salads where it absorbs balsamic vinegar and olive oil dressings—yum!
- Wild birds will also eat breadcrumbs, and you can make fat balls for the birds by mixing fat and breadcrumbs.

RECYCLE Some areas are now offering a curbside collection for garden waste, kitchen waste or both.

About 60 per cent of the average garbage can's contents are materials which can be turned into compost.

Meat and fish

People are generally advised to avoid composting meat and fish: this is primarily because of attracting rats. You can use a sealed system such as:

- the EM Bokashi system
  (see *www.emtechnologynetwork.org*)

- a worm farm (see *www.wormfarm.com*)
- a Solarcone (a proprietary sealed system that has a basket you sink into the ground and a cone above (see *www.solarcone.net*), or
- a tumbler (see *www.compostguide.com*)

It is best to seek professional advice before undertaking any large-scale recycling of cooked foods, meat, fish, cheese, etc.

The Bokashi system is not a form of composting: the kitchen scraps are fermented using bacteria, which thrive without air.

Fat from cooking can be composted (mix with plenty of paper), or, even better, mixed with breadcrumbs and seeds and poured into half a coconut shell to feed the birds.

Fruits and vegetables

Raw fruit and vegetables can go into an ordinary composting system (small amounts into a worm farm) or any of the other systems mentioned above.

Other cooked food (e.g., pasta and rice)

Similarly, put other cooked food into a Bokashi, tumbler, Solarcone, or worm farm—anything that's not accessible to rats. See *Composting: An Easy Household Guide* for more information in Resources—Books.

Fridges and Freezers

REDUCE your energy use by buying refrigerators and freezers with an Energy Star® label: Energy Star-qualified refigerators use 15% less energy than required by current federal standards and 40% less energy than the conventional models sold in 2001.

REUSE Old chest freezers are also useful as rat-proof feed stores and can be converted into composting containers or worm farms for food waste. Take to a recycling center to be reprocessed at the end of their usable life.

RECYCLE Old refrigerators and freezers contain CFCs in their coolant gases and insulation material. CFCs are extremely damaging to the ozone layer, so these old appliances must be disposed of at recycling centers, where they are sent off to be shredded at specialist facilities that recover all the useful materials and harmful gases—see **CFCs**. Modern refrigerators and freezers do not contain CFCs.

Funerals

Increasingly, more and more people want to leave the world without causing unnecessary pollution. You can now ask for a cardboard coffin, a woolen shroud, or even an ecopod. See *www.ecopod.co.uk* or *www.greenburialcouncil.org*

Furniture

RECYCLE *Sell or Donate:*

- Contact your local furniture recycling project or social services.
- Advertise it for sale locally.
- Upholsterers want good pieces to re-cover, and for their students or apprentices to practice on.
- Your municipality may arrange a 'bulky household waste' collection service.

Garden Chemicals

Avoid: Use safer and more effective biological controls in your garden and greenhouse instead of chemicals. Chemicals will kill the insects, which are more effective than anything at killing pests. There are plenty of alternatives to chemicals in the garden, many of which are now banned for use and a problem to dispose of safely.

If you have old stocks of garden chemicals to get rid of, contact your local authority for advice on disposal.

If you want 250+ tips on gardening without chemicals, see *www.organicgardentips.com*

Garden Tools—see Tools

Garden Waste
(clippings, hedge prunings, branches, etc.)

Compost: Smoke from garden bonfires is 350 times more carcinogenic than tobacco smoke, and is particularly bad for children and babies. It is far better to compost garden waste in situ.

REUSE Clippings can be sawn up for firewood or stacked as wildlife habitat areas—a fallen tree is a wildlife refuge, as is a pile of woody prunings—so if you have space, leave a corner with a wildlife pile. Amphibians, especially newts and toads, love a pile of slowly rotting wood, as do scores of beetles, some of which are becoming very scarce because of our over-tidy gardening habits.

Don't forget to save useful sticks for plants to climb up, especially peas and beans. Woody 'brash' can also be woven into uprights to make a 'fedge' (a cross between a fence and a hedge). If you do this just in front of an existing fence, wall or hedge, then not only do you create a marvelous wildlife corridor but also a space, behind which you can pile up even more woody brash or compostable materials to slowly break down. Also see **Compost**.

RECYCLE through community composting projects. Check with your local authority to see if garden waste can be picked up curbside.

Gas Tanks
These will normally be returnable to the supplier.

Glass (sheets)

REUSE Flat glass can be cut down to make smaller panes, or made into cloches for cold frames.

RECYCLE It can be taken to a household recycling center or glass merchant for recycling. Don't put it with glass bottle recycling, because it's so dangerous to handle.

Glass, along with paper and cans, is the most common item collected for recycling. This is because it is very worthwhile to collect glass, and more and more markets are opening up for it—see below.

G Glass Bottles

Recycling a glass bottle saves enough energy to light a 100-watt light bulb for four hours.

RECYCLE either at the local bottle recycling center or through curbside collection. Some areas require you to sort by color. Check with your local authority.

What happens to glass? Besides being turned back into glass bottles and jars, glass is also used for many other applications. There are many different uses for some recyclable materials, and glass is a good example.

- It is made into glasspaper or sandpaper.
- Sandblasting is an industrial abrasive system, which works even better with glass, and the great thing is that it doesn't matter what color it is. That is also true of most of the alternative uses.
- Water filtration works even better with glass than other products. Then of course there is glass fiber and fiberglass insulation. The list of alternatives is long: glass can be added to concrete (glasscrete), and to asphalt (glassphalt).
- It is used in the ceramic industry: glazes are basically a glass layer on a pot.

- It is used in hydroponic growing as a soil-less growing medium.
- Bottles are being turned into glasses: one design uses the bottle with the tapered top section cut off; another design uses the inverted top section, which is stuck on to a piece cut from the bottom of the bottle.
- Bottles can be used in house construction: mortared together on their sides, they can make translucent insulating walls.
- One entrepreneur has devised a way of slicing up bottles, heating them up, and creating flat panes of glass that can be used in making decorative glass panels.
- A new process can fuse together shards of different-colored broken glass and make a very solid worktop resembling granite called 'Ttura': see *www.eightinch.co.uk* (also see the 'Urban Ore' case study in the 'Vision for the Future' chapter at the end of this book).

Glasses (spectacles)

RECYCLE *Donate:* take to retailers for reuse in the third world. The Lions Club has a huge eyeglass recycling program—in 2005 they collected more than 5 million pairs of eyeglasses, distributing them to more than 3 million people in developing nations.

Grass Cuttings

RECYCLE *Compost:* Mix with scrunched-up paper and cardboard to help aerate, or leave them on the lawn. Buy a mulching mower, which cuts the grass up very fine to incorporate back into the soil.

Greeting Cards

REUSE Turn them into gift tags, or cut up and make new cards. Many community groups, post offices, shops, etc., collect old cards for reuse and recycling (see also **Christmas**).

Growbags

RECYCLE *Compost:* Add to your compost heap or just sprinkle on top of your soil.

Herbicides—see Chemicals

Household Cleaners—see Cleaning

Hypodermics—see Needles

Ice Cream Containers

REUSE There are lots of possibilities for storage and freezing food.

RECYCLE Check with your local authority.

Inkjet Cartridges (from computer printers)
—see also Toner Cartridges and Wireless Phones

RECYCLE There are a growing number of businesses that will buy empty inkjet cartridges—as well as fundraising options such as Cartridges for Kids (*www.cartridgesforkids.com*). Many manufacturers now include a prepaid envelope for convenient recycling. Always turn off a printer so that it parks the print head (don't just switch it off at the mains) to prevent the print head from drying up.

Jars—see Bottles and Jars

Jiffy Bags

REUSE Save for reuse.

RECYCLE *Compost:* Jiffy bags are made from brown paper and padded with shredded newsprint and are 100% compostable if too damaged to be reused.

Jigsaw Puzzles

REUSE *Donate:* Complete jigsaws can be reused by schools, playgroups, residential homes, etc., or take to thrift shops, flea markets, etc.

Junk Mail

REDUCE The Direct Marketing Association's (DMA) Mail Preference Service lets you opt out of receiving direct-mail marketing from many national companies for five years. When you register with this service, your name will be put on a 'delete' file and made available to direct-mail marketers. See: *www.the-dma.org/consumers/offmailinglist.html*

The credit bureaus offer a toll-free number that enables you to 'opt-out' of having preapproved credit offers sent to you for two years.
Call (888) 567-8688 or visit *www.optoutprescreen.com*

RECYCLE as paper.

Kitchen Foil—see Aluminum Foil

Kitchen Waste—see Food

Knitting Wool—see Wool

Lamps

RECYCLE Take to a recycling center.
Sell or Donate to charity.

Light Bulbs and Light Fittings

REDUCE Buy low-energy bulbs, especially for places where you leave the light on for long periods. Energy-efficient light bulbs last for years—I've had some going for over thirteen years now! They cost more to buy, but are well worth it.

Dimmer switches help to prolong the life of conventional (incandescent) light bulbs, and dimming your lights saves energy.

RECYCLE Some groups are now recycling light bulbs, fluorescent lights, television sets, and computer monitors. See *www.lamprecycle.org*

Linoleum

RECYCLE Real linoleum (made from linseed oil and backed with hessian) was largely supplanted many years ago by synthetic manmade floor coverings. However, you can now get all kinds of exciting linoleum made from natural ingredients, which can be shredded up and composted at the end of their useful life. See *www.themarmoleumstore.com*

Magazines

REUSE *Donate:* Dentists, doctors, and hospitals use magazines in their waiting areas; residential homes and hospices will also use them, and they are a great source of material for children's play and art classes.

RECYCLE them, either through your local curbside collection or in the newspaper bin or at the local recycling center.

Material—see Textiles

Medicines

Return unused medicine and medicine bottles to your pharmacist.

Metal

RECYCLE *Sell or Donate:* Take to a scrap metal dealer or recycling center.

Milk Bottles

REUSE *Return* glass milk bottles to your milkman/supplier.

RECYCLE Plastic milk bottles can be recycled in some areas: check with your local authority.

Mobile Phones

Wireless phones generally contain 40% metals, 40% plastics, and 20% ceramics; much of this is hazardous, including mercury and lead.

RECYCLE There are lots of ways to recycle your mobile phone:

- You can return your unwanted mobile phone handsets and accessories directly to retail outlets throughout the country. Some states have introduced legislation requiring all wireless phone providers to accept phones for reuse or recycling.
- Sprint Project Connect is a recycling program from Sprint whereby they accept all makes and models of phones, regardless of service provider. Proceeds go to K-12 programs. See *www.sprint.com/community*
- You can send your phone to Phones 4 Charity, an organization that supports a number of charities including the National Breast Cancer Foundation and the National Wildlife Federation. Nonworking phones will be recycled. See *www.phones4charity.org*
- Donate your phone to the national CALL TO PROTECT program, which provides phones to domestic-violence agencies;

phones are refurbished and become lifelines for domestic-violence survivors when faced with an emergency situation. See *www.wirelessfoundation.org*
- Recycling your mobile phone can help to reduce the impact that mining of the mineral coltan is having on the forests and wildlife of the Congo. Coltan is used to make the rare metal tantalum needed in mobile phones. See *rainforestconcern.org*

Monitors

RECYCLE TV screens and monitors contain mercury and need to be disposed of carefully: check with your local authority to see if they provide recycling for these items, or take them to a recycling center.

Many manufacturers are now offering recycling services for electronics. When you purchase a Dell computer, for example, they will recycle your old PC and monitor for free, even if they are not Dell-branded products.

REDUCE electronic product waste:
- Donate reusable electronic equipment (e.g., to schools or other nonprofit organizations).
- Buy remanufactured equipment instead of new equipment.
- Contract with suppliers to lease electronics.

Mortar

RECYCLE Reasonably clean and paint-free lime mortar and sand that comes from demolishing old brick and stone work is a good addition to acid soil. Use a length of chicken wire as a sieve to separate out pieces of rubble, then bag it up and use in the garden.

Nappies—see Diapers

Needles/Hypodermics

Dispose: If you have needles or other sharp medical equipment to dispose of, phone your local authority, doctor's office, or hospital to get advice on where to take them and how to take them in safely.

Newspaper

Recycling a three-foot stack of newspaper saves one tree.

REUSE

- Newspapers can be used for all kinds of things, from lining pets' cages to protecting floors from paint.
- If you can't use it, try donating it to local nurseries and schools for use in art and crafts.
- A thick layer of newspaper is a great 'barrier' mulch, which suppresses weeds.

RECYCLE

- Recycle curbside or at a recycling center.
- Take it to a local community group, who may shred paper for animal bedding, provided it is not contaminated with chemical spills.
- Add newspaper to the compost
- Get a Newspaper Log Roller and turn old newspapers into fireplace logs. See *www.lehmans.com*

The Office

Changing work patterns mean that more and more people are now working from home. This has the positive effect of cutting down on commuting, saving time, energy, and pollution. If you work from home, you can shop around for the best recycled office products.

REDUCE

- Use e-mail rather than paper.

- Use solar-powered calculators rather than battery-operated ones.
- Use products with a longer life, such as low-energy light bulbs, which last up to eight times longer than ordinary light bulbs and also reduce energy costs.

REUSE

- Reuse envelopes for internal mail.
- Buy envelope reuse labels, which can be purchased from charities, sometimes with your company logo printed on it.
- Use reuseable items rather than disposable ones: e.g., china cups, metal cutlery, mechanical pencils, refillable pens.
- Packaging: see if you can have a 'take-back' option on packaging, especially packing peanuts and bubble wrap (most UPS stores take packing peanuts back).

RECYCLE

- Collect stamps and milk bottle tops for charity.
- Turn scrap paper into notepads.
- Have boxes for unwanted used paper and use it in the photocopier.
- Use both sides of the paper when photocopying or producing reports.
- Use recycled paper.
- Find out whether there is an office paper collection in your area. This is high-quality paper and worthwhile collecting separately.
- Put used paper to one side for recycling.
- Have a paper shredder for confidential documents, which can then be composted or used for animal bedding or packing.
- Save used printer/toner cartridges for reuse (see under Mobile Phones and Cartridges).
- Print out documents only when you need to.

- Contact local community recyclers or charities if you are upgrading equipment—have it reused!
- Office equipment and furniture: contact a local furniture-recycling project, or sell to a second-hand shop.

Offices can be extremely wasteful places, but with a little thought and organization they can become much more sustainable. For more support in the workplace, contact Global Action Plan or visit *www.globalactionplan.com*

If each one of 10 million office workers used one fewer staple daily, there would be a saving of 705 pounds of steel a day! Use a paper clip instead!

Tips for purchasing for your home or work office
- Specify products with a recycled or reconditioned content. For wooden furniture and other timber products, this may include purchasing goods from certified, sustainable sources.
- Avoid buying disposable products and aerosols.
- Use solvent-free correction fluids and paints.
- Choose local products and materials to reduce the energy and pollution implications of transporting goods.
- Avoid over-packaged goods.
- Buy a fountain pen, or use refillable pens and highlighters.
- Consider upgrading your PCs rather than replacing them.
- Share items in occasional use, e.g., hole punchers.
- Order recycled products use stapleless paper joiners.
- Buy compostable pens made from cornstarch (called Mater-Bi), now with built-in seeds—when the pen runs out, plant it in the garden!
- Remarkable Pencils Ltd. make pens from printers, mouse pads from car tires, and lots more. See *www.remarkable.co.uk*

See *www.greenearthofficesupply.com*
www.dolphinblue.com www.sustainablegroup.net

Oil

REUSE or *Compost:* see **Cooking oil** and **Engine oil**.

Organic Waste—see Composting and Food

Oven Cleaner—see Chemicals

Packaging

REDUCE Try to avoid buying over-packaged products, especially polystyrene and plastic wrapping, which is not generally recyclable. Look for starch-based, biodegradable packaging that dissolves in water and can be composted. They are being increasingly used as packaging around fragile products.

REUSE bags—use a shopping bag or basket and buy loose products whenever possible.

RECYCLE or compost as much as you can of the cardboard and paper packaging.

Donate: If there is a mail-order business locally, they may well want your packing peanuts—see **Bubble Wrap**.

Because packaging has become such a large part of our waste, various new (and some old) ideas are around to lessen the wastage.

- One Dutch group of designers is experimenting with growing gourds into specific shapes, using plywood moulds, to produce natural packaging.
- Foamed starch polymers, made using steam instead of harmful CFC gas, are now used frequently instead of packing peanuts. The end product can then be composted after use.
- Another idea is the air box. Goods can be posted inside their own bubble of air inside a reusable plastic bag. Apparently IBM invited people to the launch of the product with an egg enclosed in the invitation!

Packed Lunches

REDUCE packaging. A survey of school waste showed that there is enormous waste, especially from packed lunches: chips, chocolates and sweets wrappers, soda drink bottles and cans. Send your child to school with refillable food and drink containers, and ask the school to get recycling facilities—see also under **Schools.**

SAVE MONEY
Producing a waste-free lunch each day can make consider-able savings. According to www.wastefreelunches.org, a typical disposable lunch includ-ing prepackaged items can cost around $4.00 while a waste-free lunch containing items repackaged from larger packages into reusable containers can cost as lit-tle as $2.65

Incredible savings! For further information and ideas on becoming environmentally friendly look at *www.waste-freelunches.org*

Paint

REDUCE Avoid toxic paints: try to use natural paints where possible.

If you purchase paints made from natural materials, plant oil extracts, and simple minerals, it is far better for your health when you are painting, and any leftover paint dries up in the can and can be composted! Natural paint in the house allows walls and wood to breathe, and natural paints smell really nice. Try real turpentine instead of turpentine substi-tute or mineral spirits—it is distilled from pine and is the best air freshener I know of!

Even if you can't smell something, it doesn't mean it doesn't affect you, and strangely enough, the less the paint smells the worse it can be.

REUSE A significant proportion of paint sold in the U.S. remains unused and is eventually disposed of, often after a period of storage. Discarded paint is awkward to dispose of and wastes valuable resources that could be used by others.

RECYCLE *Donate:* Find a home for your old unwanted paint so that it can be reused for the benefit of the community. Try community groups, playgroups, theatre groups, high school drama departments, churches, etc.—any of these may well be happy to have it.

For a list of Paint Donation/Exchange Sites in your area, see *www.earth911.org*

Dispose: Some old paints contain lead and other dangerous substances and should be taken to a recycling center for safe disposal.

Paper—see also Newspaper

P

> *Every day American businesses generate enough paper to circle the earth 20 times!*

REUSE
- Make the best use of paper.
- Use both sides of the paper.
- Make a scrap paper pad.
- Buy recycled paper.

RECYCLE all your clean flat paper. If paper is recycled the amount of waste going to landfill is cut and less timber is used. Managing our insatiable demand for timber should reduce the need to clear old-growth forests, which are rich in biodiversity.

Compost soiled and crumpled paper.

Americans use more than 67 million tons of paper per year, or over 400 pounds per person.

Paper Towels

BUY RECYCLED: always use paper towels made from recycled paper.

RECYCLE Put used paper towels (and the cardboard roll) in the compost.

Peat

REDUCE/ *Avoid* Our precious peat bogs are being destroyed by peat extraction. Peat bogs take thousands of years to form and are a unique ecosystem. At the same time as we are destroying peat bogs, we are landfilling or burning materials (especially from our gardens) that we can compost to make a wonderful peat substitute.

REUSE If you have any peat from bought-in plants, it can be added to the compost heap or just spread in the garden.

Pesticides—see Garden Chemicals

Photographic Chemicals

Donate: These contain silver, which is worth reclaiming—try asking your local photography shop.

Dispose: Check with your local authority about household hazardous waste (HHW) disposal, and remember:
• Keep HHW products separate (do not mix).
• Bring products in their original containers when possible.
• Seal products to prevent leaks and spills.
• Keep products away from the driver and passengers, i.e., in a trunk, truck bed, or trailer.
• Keep children and pets away from collection sites and events.

Pillows—see Bedding

Plastics

360 million plastic bottles were recycled in 2002.

REDUCE It may be impossible to avoid plastics, but we can at least try to minimize the amount of plastic we use and throw away by:
• Refusing plastic bags
• Refilling containers
• Purchasing alternative products
• Buying products in glass bottles where possible

RECYCLE Plastics will undoubtedly be more widely recycled when more facilities for dealing with mixed plastics are built. Some municipalities collect mixed plastics, including plastic film but excluding expanded polystyrene. Areas that collect for recycling concentrate on plastic bottles because they are made of the highest-value plastic. Your local recycling center should have a plastic bottle collection dumpster so that the most dedicated recycler can save up plastic bottles to drop off. However, at the moment even the most diehard recyclers and avoiders of packaging and waste are still likely to be filling their garbage cans with plastic.

New Uses for Recycled Plastic
There are masses of applications for recycled plastic in contemporary design products—including furniture, clothing, lamps, screens, construction, flooring, etc., either as single plastics or even as mixed plastics fused together.

Designers are also coming up with new uses for plastic objects: for instance, a plastic fishing float turned into a light, and plastic bottles linked together to make a floating lounger for use in the swimming pool. Another designer uses a group of plastic milk bottles with lights in and it makes a surprisingly elegant light with subtle diffusion.

Plastic Bottles

Recycling a single plastic bottle can conserve enough energy to light a 60W lightbulb for up to 6 hours.

There are lots of different types of plastic—if you are interested in finding out a bit more, see the chart later on in this section. The majority of plastic bottles are made from PET or HDPE—the most valuable and worthwhile plastics to recycle.

RECYCLE Make sure you squash them (remove the tops first). Plastic bottles can be made into fleeces (see *www.patagonia.com*).

REUSE

• Use as a mini-cloche to protect plants.
• You can utilize the whole bottle to make a self-watering system. Cut the bottle in half and fill the bottom half with water. Turn the top half upside down and fill with compost and your plant. Put the top half into the bottom. You can then regulate the water by loosening or tightening the top.

Plastic Shopping Bags

REDUCE / *Refuse* bags:

- Try the impossible and avoid plastic as much as you can.
- Take your own! Keep a few plastic bags in your pockets so that you don't need to take home yet another plastic bag.

> *We use eight billion plastic bags each year—*
> *more than 300 for every household.*

- Say 'no' to plastic bags and 'yes' to paper.
- Take a shopping basket or a cloth bag with you when you go shopping.
- Take a 'plastic bag for life'.
- Some supermarkets now have 'degradable' bags (made from petrochemicals) that go brittle after a while and fall apart. A better solution is the 'compostable' bag, available in some retail outlets.

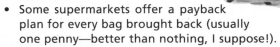

- Some supermarkets offer a payback plan for every bag brought back (usually one penny—better than nothing, I suppose!).

Since the Irish government put a tax on plastic bags, there has been a 95% reduction in bag use, and the problems with them littering the streets disappeared overnight.

REUSE

Although they are a problem, plastic bags also have masses of uses, as you can use them over and over again, e.g.:

- Scrunched up instead of bubble wrap (cheaper).
- For packed lunches
- For freezing

- When packing your suitcase
- Reuse old plastic bags rather than buying rolls of new ones

RECYCLE Use in-store recycling bins, or offer them to shops that don't have their own bags, such as thrift shops and health stores.

Plastic Cups

REDUCE Buy a large inexpensive set of glasses and keep them on hand for entertaining, or rent a few cases from a caterer.

Plastic Trays (around vegetables, fruit, etc.)

REDUCE Avoid where possible—try to buy fruit and vegetables without this packaging—you could resort to unwrapping it at the checkout and leaving it for the store to dispose of as shoppers in Germany are starting to do.

REUSE as seed trays, etc.

Plastic Yogurt Cups

Thick or thin? Some manufacturers have made their cups as thin as possible to minimize the plastic used and strengthened them with an outer wrapping of cardboard, which can be removed for composting or recycling.

A few manufacturers have taken the opposite approach and have put their yogurt in sturdy reusable pots. However, there are only so many you can use!

REUSE as seed pots, as paint pots, for children's play.

Plastic Packaging

Over 60% of the total plastic waste comes from packaging, which is typically thrown away within one year of sale.

80% of our plastic waste ends up in landfill.

Hard polystyrene preformed packaging (e.g., used to protect electrical appliances)

Dispose: Try to get the suppliers to take it back; otherwise you will have to put it out for the rubbish collection.

What happens to polystyrene?

Polystyrene can be made into new products including as a replacement for hardwood, which is suitable for garden furniture, window frames, and picture frames.

Expanded Polystyrene (EPS)

This is the soft cushioning plastic that many goods come wrapped in, e.g., refrigerators, televisions, computers, and goods sent through the mail. It is recyclable, although it is really only feasible for the trade to recycle it. In theory, the supplier of the goods should take back any packaging, and we should all be insisting that they do just that.

REDUCE There is a compostable version called Eco-Foam made from corn starch. See also **Biodegradable Plastics** below.

REUSE If you know anyone who has a mail-order business or runs a shop where they need to pack fragile items, they might be happy to use this kind of packaging.

Plastic Wrap

RECYCLE With so many different types of plastic used in packaging, each with its own symbol, is it any wonder that people get confused by what they can and cannot recycle?

There are about 50 different types of plastic. *www.recoup.org* gives information on plastic and plastic products.

Frequently Asked Questions

What do the codes mean?

The most common forms of plastic packaging found in the home are often marked with a code. This helps us to know which plastic is which. The code can be either a number or letters, and is usually found in or with a recycling sign, but you may still have difficulty in finding somewhere to recycle plastic near your home.

What do the numbers mean?

- 1 or PET = Polyethylene terephthalate (e.g., soda drink bottles and water bottles)
- 2 or HDPE = High-density polyethylene (e.g., milk bottles, detergent, and oil bottles)
- 3 or PVC = Polyvinyl chloride (e.g., food trays, detergent bottles, food wrap, vegetable oil bottles, blister packaging, pipes)
- 4 or LDPE = Low-density polyethylene (e.g., plastic bags, bin liners, sandwich/bread bags, six-pack rings)
- 5 or PP = Polypropylene (e.g., margarine tubs, straws, refrigerated containers, screw-on bottle tops/lids, some carpets, some food wrap)
- 6 or PS = Polystyrene (e.g., yogurt cups, styrofoam cups, throwaway utensils, meat packing, packaging chips)
- 7 other = Polycarbonate, acrylic, ABS, mixed/multi-layer plastic.

Numbers 1 and 2 are the most commonly recycled plastics at the moment. Hopefully in the future we will be able to recycle them all.

What is plastic made from?
Plastics are made from oil—usually mineral oil (petroleum), although plastics made from plant material are becoming more common.

Are there any alternatives?
Biodegradable Plastics: Plastics made from plant materials like corn starch are useful as they are fully biodegradable and can be composted:

- These bags can be used for kitchen waste to keep the bin clean and to contain kitchen waste for compost collection rounds.
- They are also used as dog poo bags.

Bioplastics are also used for compostable plates and cutlery. The maize plants at the Eden Project are being mulched with maize cutlery! In Australia, kangaroos and other animals soon eat biodegradable fast-food boxes tossed out of the car, or they biodegrade naturally—perhaps not the most elegant of solutions, but at least it cuts down on plastic litter. See *www.biopolymer.net*

Is plastic recycling really worthwhile?

> *25 recycled PET bottles can be used
> to make an adult's fleece jacket.*

Genuine recycling, where there is no loss of quality and materials can be endlessly 'upcycled' into similar or better products, is viable. However, where plastics are mixed they can only be 'downcycled'; this should really only be seen as a short-term solution as everything produced should be either compostable at the end of its useful life or endlessly recyclable without loss of quality. Having said that, recycling plastic can be cost-effective. Municipalities currently spend millions every year on the collection and disposal of plastics. Through effective collection plans they can sell plastics and generate income instead. Usually when plastic is recycled it is changed into another type of item. For example, soda bottles (PET bottles) can be recycled into insulating material for synthetic fleece jackets, or back into recycled bottles.

There are some plastics factories that can take mixed plastics. Old plastics are shredded and mixed together then heated. The plastics with the lowest melting temperature fuse around the unmelted plastics, and the whole lot is extruded to form a variety of chunky shapes, posts, planks, slabs, etc. Shredded tires can be added to give a nonslip surface, and woodchips can be added, which helps make the final product lighter. The end products have a number of uses—canal bank strengthening, nonslip bicycle paths, garden furniture, planters— and more uses are being found all the time.

Postcards

RECYCLE *Donate:* Old postcards can be donated to museums. Do an Internet search for a museum appropriate to the postcard subject and contact them.

Potato Chip Bags

Although chip bags and other similar bags carry a recycling symbol, this is relevant only to the plastic scraps generated during the process of making the bags in the factory. You cannot recycle chip bags at present (see also under **Children**).

Printer Cartridges—see Toner Cartridges

RECYCLE *Donate:* An Internet search will provide a list of charities that accept donations of used printer cartridges. (Some for-profit firms will purchase empty cartridges.)

Quilts—see Clothing

Radiators
RECYCLE Take to a recycling center.

Radios—see Electrical Appliances

Rags
REUSE for cleaning, paint, or car rags, or recycle for paper-making, etc.—see **Textiles**.

Rain Boots
REUSE Cut down rain boots to use as slip-ons. Plant things in them.

RECYCLE *Donate* to thrift shops—in pairs!

Rechargeable Batteries—see Batteries

Record Players—see Electrical Appliances

Use your granny's wind-up—great for picnics!

Records, Tapes
RECYCLE *Sell or Donate* to thrift shops.

Refrigerators and Freezers—see Fridges and Freezers

Rent

If you only need something occasionally, why not rent it, rather than having to store, repair and eventually dispose of it?

Sanitary Protection

Never flush down the toilet. Choose organic unbleached tampons and sanitary towels with minimum packaging. Use alternative sanitary protection—contact the Women's Environmental Network for more information.
See *www.wencal.org*

Sawdust

REUSE Use for pet cages, or add in small quantities to compost heaps.

Schools—also see 'Children'

Where better to start putting across the three Rs (Reduce, Reuse, and Recycle, of course!) than at school!

There are all kinds of initiatives, from aluminum can recycling for school fundraising to whole school eco-makeovers. Many local authorities are promoting the three Rs either by going into schools themselves, by sponsoring theater groups or specialists to work with the children, or by doing a 'waste audit.' During a waste audit, all the waste in the school is collected for a week and then emptied out on a huge piece of tarpaulin spread out in the gym or on the playing field. Everything is sorted into categories, and the children can see how much waste is going on and start to think about ways to reduce it. Children love to recycle—is your local school doing its bit?

The Go Green Initiative offers a Public Relations Kit For Schools created to help you publicize your Go Green Initiative program and plans with teachers, parents, school board members, the media, etc. See *www.gogreeninitiative.org*

Paper Recycles, the Website of The Paper Industry Association Council has a comprehensive guide to starting a recycling program in your school. See *www.paperrecycles.org*

Look for local retailers to partner with your school, or other fundraising/recycling programs. One Texas supermarket chain, H-E-B, has a program whereby a school can sign up to collect H-E-B plastic grocery bags and earn money for every pound accumulated. The bags are then turned into trash bags, which can be purchased at H-E-B.

Shoes

RECYCLE *Donate or Reuse:* Thrift shops and some clothing banks accept shoes in good condition—in pairs!

REUSE There are a number of charities that send your used sneakers to impoverished places with little access to athletic shoes. Shoe4Africa collects running shoes and ships them to East Africa to encourage sport. The first pair of Shoe4Africa shoes to be donated back in 1995 went to Mark Wendot Yatich, then an unknown runner—he went on to win the Los Angeles Marathon and run 2:09. Another runner to get shoes that year was Japheth Kimutai, who three years later won the Commonwealth Games 800m gold medal.
See *www.tanser.org*

Donate your sneakers! There are a number of options for donating old sneakers. Nike has a fantastic recycling program called Reuse-A-Shoe, which is working to close the loop on the life cycle of literally millions of pairs of old, worn-out, or otherwise unusable athletic shoe material. Nike collects

worn-out athletic shoes of any brand, not just Nike, and recycles them into a material that is used to make new soccer and football fields, tennis and basketball courts, running tracks, and playground surfaces around the world.
See *www.nikereuseashoe.com*

Soap
RECYCLE You can buy soap presses that make new bars, and even chop them up to make a liquid soap.

Spectacles—see Glasses

Stamps
RECYCLE *Compost or Donate* to thrift shops.
Sell to collectors or specialist shops.

Strollers, Wheelchairs, and Cots
RECYCLE *Sell or Donate:* Advertise locally or contact your local social services.

Telephone Directories
REUSE Great for raising the height of your computer monitor!

RECYCLE

- Tear them in half and add to your compost bin. (That's what I do. OK—I do it a page at a time!)
- Shred up for animal bedding. You may have a community project or small business near you that will do this.
- Telephone directories can go into magazine/newspaper recycling banks, or be collected through your curbside recycling program.

Textiles—see also Clothing, Curtains

RECYCLE *Sell or Donate:* Put in donation boxes. Good-condition textiles are accepted by thrift shops.

What happens to old textiles?

There is an increasing number of entrepreneurial businesses that take used clothing and reinvent them as new 'one-off' pieces, or utilize the fabric for new designs altogether. This is an extension of the philosophy of 'make do and mend,' long practiced by skilled seamstresses with the design flair to crate a natty new outfit from a bag of tag-sale leftovers. For many who sell their handiwork through craft shops, it is a money-earning hobby; for a very few it may provide a livelihood.

Tiles

RECYCLE Old tiles can be disposed of at a recycling center. *Sell:* Good clean tiles in reasonable quantities can be sold: advertise locally or take to an architectural reclamation yard or recycling center. Interesting old tiles can also be sold through small ads, garage sales, etc.

Timber (Wood)

REUSE wherever possible, otherwise take to a recycling center.

RECYCLE Offcuts can be used for woodburning stoves. Tanalised wood, blockboard, plywood, fiberboard, and chipboard contain toxic substances, and should not be burned. However, most of them can be recycled back into chipboard. *Sell or Donate:* Good-quality wood is always useful and can be resold. Some communities now have wood reuse facilities. See also *www.recycle-it.org*

In the U.S., nearly six million tons of wood waste (e.g., urban wood waste, woody debris from suburban land clearing, and rural forestry residuals) were generated in 2003 according to the EPA. In fact, wood comprises the largest percentage of the residential construction and demolition debris waste stream—approximately 40 to 50 percent of residential new construction debris—according to the National Association of Home Builders Research Center.

Richard Mehmed runs a wood recycling project in Brighton and Hove in the UK. Community wood projects like these can rescue enormous quantities of wood for reuse. His team collects wood from construction sites and sells it on for home-improvement projects and other uses. Even though much of the wood collected is not suitable for reuse, it can be cut up for firewood and kindling. Builders are slowly realizing that their waste wood is a resource for others. For more information on Richard Mehmed's project, see *www.community woodrecycling.org.uk.*

Tin Cans—see Cans

Tin cans are in fact made mostly of steel.

Tires

REDUCE Try to buy reconditioned tires where available and carry out regular maintenance checks, such as tire pressure, to extend the tires' life.

REUSE Scrap tires make excellent compost bins or worm farms (place several tires one above the other), plant holders when filled with soil (very good for potatoes!), children's swings and play equipment, and boat fenders.

RECYCLE The metal rim, once it has been separated from the tire, can be recycled at recycling centers. Most garages will take unwanted tires for recycling or safe disposal. Unwanted tires must not be placed in your household trash.

What happens to old tires?

They can be ground up to make playground surfaces and mixed with some plastics—see **Plastics**. There is even a method for adding microorganisms (they found sulphur-eating bacteria in the hot springs in Yellowstone Park), which eat up the sulphur used in the vulcanization process. This makes the rest of the tire easier to recycle.

Toner Cartridges—see also Inkjet Cartridges

Each year, millions of empty toner cartridges are thrown in the trash, destined for landfills and incinerators.

RECYCLE Recycling at Work, a campaign of the National Office Paper Recycling Project in partnership with four of its sponsors (Canon, Hewlett-Packard, Lexmark, and Xerox), has developed a comprehensive brochure on toner-cartridge recycling. Information includes how to recycle empty toner cartridges, where to recycle the cartridge, what is done with the materials that are returned to the manufacturer, and sponsor companies' contact information for further inquiries. For more information and to download the brochure, go to *www.usmayors.org/uscm/recycle/toner.htm*

Tools

RECYCLE *Sell:* You can often sell tools at garage sales.

Toys and Games

REDUCE Use your local toy library if you have one.

RECYCLE *Sell or Donate* to friends, playgroups, residential homes, hospitals, thrift shops, church groups, garage sales, etc.

Vending Cups

Billions of plastic cups are thrown away every year.

REUSE Wash out and reuse for parties, or put a hole in the bottom and use for growing seedlings and small plants.

Water

REDUCE It's strange that some people still have an aversion to recycling when our most basic commodity, water, is being constantly recycled all the time. New housing constantly increases the demand for water, and for that reason a range of water-saving measures are often included in newly built houses. Whatever the age of your house, you can do your bit to conserve water.

- Have a shower rather than a bath, but remember that a 'power shower' can use as much water as a bath if run for five minutes.
- Turn off the tap when brushing your teeth.
- Don't wash dishes with running water.
- Install taps that act like showers, instead of delivering a solid stream.
- Install dual-flush toilets.
- Put a brick in your toilet tank so that it uses less water.
- Water your garden at night so the water doesn't evaporate but soaks in.
- Get rain barrels and save rainwater.
- Fit devices to downspouts and gutters to capture water— better for plants than chlorinated tap water.
- Compost—a garden with plenty of humus in the soil from adding compost holds rainfall better and needs less watering.

RECYCLE
• You can divert your sink and bath water to use in the garden.

Wax Paper
RECYCLE *Compost:* It is compostable, but does take quite a time to break down, so rip it up and scrunch it first.

Wood—see Timber

Woody Prunings
Pile up in a corner of your garden to slowly rot down. In the meantime it will be a refuge for amphibians and beetles—great for keeping the pests down in the garden.

Wool
RECYCLE *Compost* if moth-eaten or too old to reuse.
Donate to quilting clubs, residential homes, thrift shops.

Workplace
• Take ideas from this book into your place of work.
• Talk to your manager or boss about putting into practice some money-saving measures (you're sure to get a favorable reaction if you put it like that!).
• Suggest that everyone is asked for their ideas about how to reduce waste.
• Have boxes for paper used only on one side for photocopying less-important documents, etc.
• Have a box for collecting ink cartridges.
• Get a worm farm for packed lunch waste, tea bags, coffee grounds, etc.
• Look into buying products made from recycled materials.
• Volunteer to do some research.

- Volunteer to collect certain items to take to the local recycling center.

Writing paper

REUSE Always buy recycled paper, and use both sides.

RECYCLE / *Compost* after use.

Yellow Pages—see Telephone Directories

Yogurt Cups—see Plastics

Zero Waste

What's left over! You can compost your hair shirt now, and use your garbage can as a worm farm!

Chapter 4

What can I do?

There's lots you can do to make a difference:

Easy

Lighten your garbage can—take out everything that can be composted and use your current recycling service. Don't use that plastic box to store toys or tools: it's for recycling! Most of us now have some sort of curbside program. Read the information that comes with it, or contact your local authority for more information. If you have Internet access, look on your municipality's Website.

- Avoid over-packaging. Do you need to buy items individually wrapped? If so, is the wrapping material made from recycled materials? Could you buy the same product made from recycled materials?
- Take a bag when you go shopping—put plastic shopping bags in your pockets so you always have some handy.
- Contact your local authority or recycling group before you clear out the garage or attic and see what you can take (and where) for reuse or recycling. See **Bulky Refuse** in the A-Z list, or individual headings.
- Use your consumer power in the workplace too. For example, nearly every office has a photocopier. Does it use recycled paper? Has it ever been tried? Do you collect paper used only on one side for reuse? Tell your boss how the business can save money by recycling
- Choose longer-life, energy-efficient, solar-powered, and rechargeable products
- Try out a low-energy light bulb.
- Give up burning trash.

- Buy recycled products, e.g., recycled toilet paper, kitchen rolls, tissues, refuse sacks, writing paper and envelopes. Switch to recycled paper in your printer.
- Use proper cups, plates, and cutlery rather than plastic or paper disposable items.
- Keep asking questions at your local store about the availability of recycled products. Congratulate the store manager when new recycled content product ranges are stocked.
- Shop at thrift shops.
- Help spread the Reduce, Reuse, Recycle message (the three Rs).

A bit more effort

Can anyone else use your cast-offs? Try your local playgroup, school, charities, community group, community hall, or social services.

- Compost all your garden and kitchen waste—see the **Compost** section for details on this.
- Collect plastic bottles for recycling.
- Look at what you are currently throwing away (e.g., plastic bottles, aluminum foil, clothes, boots and shoes, etc.), and see if you can find places locally to take them: see the A-Z guide and contact your local authority and/or recycling group for more information and help.
- Buy remanufactured printer cartridges for home or workplace computers, and return spent cartridges for recycling. (See the A-Z list.)
- Buy loose fruit and vegetables—refuse excess packaging.
- Buy local produce. Use your local shops and services.
- Plan any building or renovation project with recycling in mind—advertise materials you will have in advance. Educate your builders. Remember that you can sell metals—lead and copper are especially valuable. Cables contain the highest grade copper.
- Buy reclaimed materials for building projects. Buy fixtures and fittings from salvage yards.

- Furniture and household goods can go to people on low incomes.
- Switch all your light bulbs to low-energy ones.
- Buy a paper shredder and use the shreddings for pet bedding. Then you can compost soiled bedding (with your kitchen waste, naturally).
- Search the Web for recycled goods—check out the Websites in the A-Z Guide as a starting point.

Thousands of cans of trash are thrown away every minute.

Go the whole hog!

Volunteer to help your local recycling or composting project.

- Find out even more about waste minimization, composting, reuse and recycling.
- Find out if you can be involved in going into schools to spread the message—contact *www.paperrecycles.org* or talk to your local school district.
- Go to community meetings and ask why they are not doing even more.
- Become a collector of those 'fringe' recyclable items that charities collect, such as corks, metal foil, printer cartridges, jumble, books, bric-a-brac, etc.
- Start your own resource center or recycling/composting project.
- Take part in a Master Composter training program.
- Help your local authority promote composting in the community; contact your local recycling officer and see if there are any opportunities available locally.
- Be a 'positive' shopper—try to buy only things that are grown locally, produced locally, or are fair-traded and/or organic. Think every time you buy something. What's it

made of? Can it be composted, or reused or recycled at the end of its life? Has it harmed anyone or the environment during its production? Should we be making anything that has a negative impact on the planet? Consider this quote from *Cradle to Cradle* by William McDonough and Michael Braungart:

"All the ants on the planet, taken together, have a biomass greater than that of humans. Yet their productiveness nourishes plants, animals and soil. Human industry has been in full swing for little over a century yet it has brought a decline in almost every ecosystem on the planet. Nature doesn't have a design problem. People do." (See *www.mbdc.com*)

We'll have a look at this some more in the next chapter.

Chapter 5

A vision for the future

In the future, people may not be talking about 'waste': resources will be so valuable that we will conserve them much more carefully.

Zero Waste

'Zero waste' is also a concept catching on in many places. New Zealand and Australia already have whole districts and states declaring themselves advocates of zero waste. In the UK, Wales has declared itself a zero-waste zone.

Zero Waste is a philosophy and a design principle for the 21st century. It includes 'recycling' but goes beyond this by taking a 'whole system' approach to the vast flow of resources and waste through human society. Zero Waste maximizes recycling, minimizes waste, reduces consumption, and ensures that products are made to be reused, repaired, or recycled back into nature or the marketplace.' See *www.zerowaste.com* and *www.grrn.org*

A new way of thinking

If things can't be recycled, repaired, reused, or composted, then should they be produced in the first place? Already there are plenty of examples of substituting products with those made from recyclable materials: e.g., the ubiquitous fast-food polystyrene box can now be made out of natural biodegradable material. In Australia the kangaroos eat the packaging! I've seen a frisbee in Brighton made from hemp oil.

As toxic materials like PVC become outlawed they will eventually cease to be in the 'waste stream,' which will then of course become a 'clean resource stream.' The ultimate goal is for the cycles to mimic natural cycles as far as possible, rather than having broken cycles (as we do now), which mean more and more exploitation of our environment.

Inspiration

A resource park: Urban Ore in California

Instead of having waste tips, we should be developing resource parks. This is what Dan Knapp at 'Urban Ore Inc.' in Berkeley, California, has done. Dan spent a happy period of his life as a scavenger at a landfill site. While there, he realized that all the discards could be put into just twelve categories: paper, metal, glass, plastic, textiles, chemical, putrescible, wood, ceramic, soils, plants, and reusable.

The Urban Ore operation collects source-separated reusable items, recyclables, organics, and residuals. Reusable items are taken for refurbishment or repair and are sold on site. This part of the operation includes a training program. The recyclable materials are sorted, baled up, etc., for sale. Some of these are reprocessed on site. For instance, a local inventor has figured out a way of fusing together mixed crushed glass, which is made into kitchen worktops and resembles granite. These are sold at over $100 per square foot.

There are also artists working on site retrieving interesting items to be made or incorporated into artwork. Wood for reuse or for chipping is taken next, then all plant material and putrescibles for composting. Chemical wastes are another stage of the operation, sorted into their chemical families wherever possible. The residuals are then sorted and picked over. Any items that can be salvaged at this stage are taken out, e.g., cardboard, paper, cans, etc. Finally, this residual stream is also composted in a separate operation. When it's stable and sanitized, it's landfilled. The landfill site is different from any other. It has no smell and no flocks of seagulls, vultures, or crows. Obviously in time it's hoped that the residual part of the operation will dwindle to as near zero as possible.

Imagine having 'resource centers' like this, where you could take the family for a good day out! They are being planned in some places now, with educational facilities, small innovative business enterprises, and linked into the local food chain that will sell local food products and serve local food in the café. Then you could 'shop till you drop' with a clean conscience.

Alameda County, the home of Urban Ore, won't collect any rubbish that is deemed recyclable!

In the Netherlands they have curbside shoe collections, and old computers are returned to manufacturers.

A town: Curitiba in Brazil

Curitiba was a very fast-growing city in the early 1960s, and a group of architects managed to persuade the mayor that the city needed some careful planning. A competition was organized, and the mayor, Jaime Lerner, started to put his visionary ideas into action. One of these ideas was to minimize waste.

Curitiba's citizens now separate their garbage into just two categories—organic and inorganic—for pick-up by two kinds of vehicles. Poor families in squatter settlements that are unreachable by trucks bring their garbage bags to local centers where they can exchange them for bus tickets or for eggs, milk, oranges, and potatoes, all bought from outlying farms.

The garbage goes to a plant (itself built of recycled materials) that employs people to separate bottles from cans and from plastics. The workers are handicapped people, recent immigrants, and alcoholics.

Recovered materials are sold to local industries. Styrofoam is shredded to stuff quilting for the poor. The recycling program costs no more than the old landfill, but the city is cleaner, there are more jobs, farmers are supported, and the poor get food and transportation. Curitiba recycles two-thirds of its garbage—one of the highest rates of any city, north or south.

For more information about this truly amazing city, see *www.dismantle.org*

In researching this book, it has been fascinating to see all the small entrepreneurs being innovative with the materials that we discard. Much of the inspiration for this has come from the so called 'third world,' where of course virtually anything thrown away is seized upon and used to make something else:

- Toy vehicles in Africa made from coat-hangers and old tins
- Sandals with tire tread soles, even hammocks made from tires
- Plastic containers of all sorts used for water containers (being lighter than the traditional ceramic)
- Earrings made from old typewriter keys (and flip-flops!)
- Beaded anti-fly door screen made of strings of beads from washed-up flip-flops
- Cufflinks from Scrabble pieces
- Clothing from old photo negatives and plastic bags, even old CDs
- Baskets woven from telephone cable and old plastic bags— very colorful
- Bags from metro fabric, carpets, and tires
- Whole houses from tires, glass bottles, and tin cans

And these are some incredible artworks from the discards of our society—worthy of a lavishly illustrated book!

> *In Switzerland, tax from bottle manufacturers*
> *is paid to communities that recycle.*

An individual: The man who throws nothing away

There's a man in Washington state named Van Calvez who has not thrown anything away for 15 years. Well, hardly any-thing— now and again he has to do it, if only to stop drawing attention to himself! What started as a hobby has now become his career. By carefully thinking about what he is buying in the first place, and by recycling and reuse he has managed over fif-teen years to reduce his waste stream so much that it fits into just four boxes in his home. This forms a part of the display materials that he travels around with. Despite the fact that he stockpiles stuff the rest of us would hurry to hurl, he's not what the psychiatric field would call a hoarder. 'I think our society is addictive and compulsive anyway. So if I'm doing something obsessive, that's good, that's OK with me.'

'Garbage is a relatively new concept,' he says. 'A hundred years ago there was very little waste at all.'

Van Calvez is maybe a crazy visionary, but even his wife has started hoarding the polystyrene clamshell packaging that she cannot bring herself to throw away. I know how she feels: I've got two bags of it myself!

Over to you

This book doesn't claim to have all the answers—maybe you can fill in some of the gaps?! If it makes you pause for thought and take a look at what you throw away, like Van Calvez did (he tipped the whole garbage can out on his kitchen floor and categorized everything!), then it has achieved its purpose.

If we all stop every now and then to wonder where all these things come from and where they are going, maybe we will start to make better choices about what we buy and what we do with it at the end of its useful life (for us). We can stop, or at least diminish, the gigantic flow of discarded materials that go into holes in the ground or up in smoke. We can have fun doing it, and at the same time feel good about making a real contribution to improving our environment.

Resources

Organizations

Alliance for Beverage Cartons and the Environement
www.drinkscartons.com

Community Composting Network
www.communitycompost.org

Earth 911 *www.earth911.org*

Earthday Network *www.earthday.net*

Ecological Footprint Quiz *www.myfootprint.org*

EPA: Municipal Solid Waste *www.epa.gov/msw/recycle*

Go Green Initiative *www.gogreeninitiative.org*

GrassRoots Recycling Network *www.grrn.org*

Green Burial Council *www.greenburialcouncil.org*

Green Energy Choice *www.greenenergychoice.com*

Lamprecycle.org *www.lamprecycle.org*

MBDC: William McDonough and Michael Braungart
www.mbdc.com

Money to Schools *www.moneytoschools.com*

National Biodiesel Board *www.biodiesel.org*

National Recycling Coalition *www.nrc-recycle.org*

Paper Industry Association Council *www.paperrecycles.org*

Rechargeable Battery Recycling Corporation
www.rbrc.org

Recycles.Org Nonprofit Recycling Network
www.recycles.org

Shoe4Africa *www.tanser.org*

Sound Resource Management Group *www.zerowaste.com*

Women's Environmental Network *www.wencal.org*

World Wide Fund for Nature *www.panda.org*

Books

Astonishing Art with Recycled Rubbish: Splatter! Splodge! Splash! by Susan Martineau and Martin Ursell, b small publishing, $9.95

Belair World of Display: The Art of Recycling (A World of Display Series) by Hilary Ansell, Belair Publications, $28.95

Beyond Recycling: A Re-users Guide by Kathy Stein. 336 Practical Tips; Save Money and Protect the Environment, Clear Light Publishers, $14.95

Cash for Your Trash: Scrap Recycling in America by Carl A. Zimring, Rutgers University Press, $39.95

The Cast-off Recast: Recycling and the Creative Transformation of Mass-produced Objects by Timothy Corrigan Correll, Patrick Arthur Polk, UCLA Press, $50.00

Cradle to Cradle: Remaking the way we make things by W. McDonough, Rodale Books, $16.50

Crafty Containers from Recycled Materials by Lois Walpole, Search Press, $17.95

Creative Recycling in Embroidery by Val Holmes, Batsford, $24.95

Fun With Recycling: 50 Great Things for Kids to Make from Junk by Marion Elliot, Southwater, $12.95

Garbage and Recycling by Rosie Harlow, Kingfisher, $7.95

Recycle!: A Handbook for Kids by Gail Gibbons, Little, Brown Young Readers, $7.99

Rescue Mission Planet Earth by Boutros Bourtos Ghali, a children's edition of Agenda 21, Kingfisher Books, $9.95

Retro Revamp: Funky Projects from Handbags to Housewares by Jennifer Knapp, Chronicle Books, $12.50

Things Reconstructed by David Kemp. Art from found and discarded objects, Alison Hodge Publishers, $19.93

The New Natural House Book by David Pearson, Fireside, $24.95

The Toilet Papers: Recycling Waste and Conserving Water by Sim Van der Ryn, Chelsea Green Publishing, $14.00

The Total Beauty of Sustainable Products by Edwin Datschefski, RotoVision, $54.50

The Treasure of Trash: A Recycling Story by Linda Mandel, Avery Publishing Group, $10.00

Urban Recycling and the Search for Sustainable Community Development by Adam S. Weinberg, David N. Pellow, Allan Schnaiberg, Rutgers University Press, $55.00

Where Does Rubbish Go by S. Tahta, Usborne Pocket Science Series, $18.80

Worms Eat My Garbage: How to Set Up and Maintain a Worm Composting System by Mary Appelhof, Flower Press, $12.95